How To DRAW!®

Cool Wheels

Illustrated by
Mike Gardner

SUPPLIES

- NUMBER 2 PENCILS
- SOFT ERASER
- COLORED PENCILS
- MARKERS OR CRAYONS

HELPFUL HINTS

1. Take your time with steps 1 and 2.
Following the first steps carefully will make the final steps easier. The first two steps create a foundation of the vehicle body—much like the frame of a house forms the foundation of the rest of the building. Next comes the fun part: creating the smooth, clean outline drawing of the car, and adding all the finishing touches, details, shading, and color.

2. Always keep your pencil lines light and soft.
This will make your guidelines easier to erase when you no longer need them.

3. Don't be afraid to erase.
It usually takes a lot of drawing and erasing before you will be satisfied with the way your drawing looks.

4. Add details at the end.
Shading and finishing touches should be the last step *after* you have blended and refined all the shapes.

5. Remember: Practice makes perfect.
Don't be discouraged if you don't get the hang of it right away. Just keep drawing, erasing, and redrawing until you do.

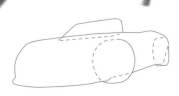

Lamborghini

The Lamborghini is an Italian car known for its sleek, exotic designs. Its modern dome body shape creates the feeling that it could take off into outer space.

 Erase any unwanted lines. Draw wheel wells, mirror, door, and air intakes. Draw the window and windshield.

Draw the shapes of the canopy, body, and the two visible tires. Draw through the shapes where they overlap.

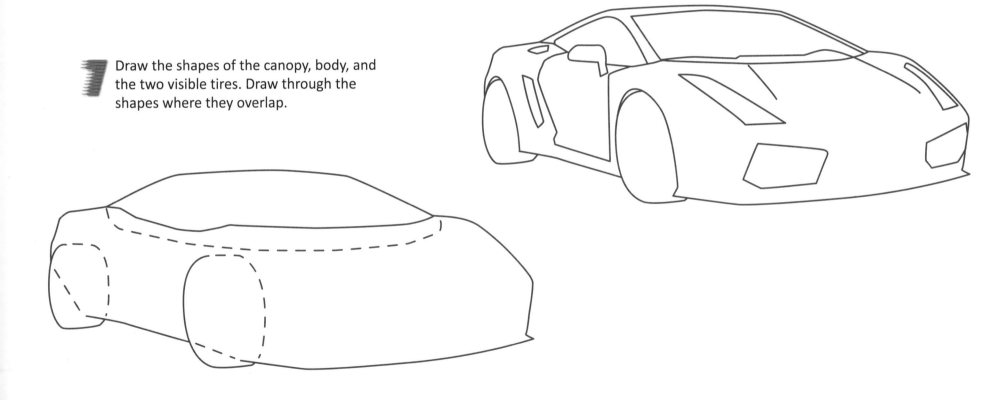

3 Finish tire and rim details. Use lines to show all the angular features of this car. Draw in the lights and glass.

4 Choose a white and black combo for this sleek looking Lamborghini. Go with black rims and tinted glass for that cool look.

Ferrari

Designed by Italian Sports Car Racer Enzo Ferrari, it's one of the fastest cars ever. Winner of countless Formula One races, this exotic red streak is a favorite of almost anyone who loves cars.

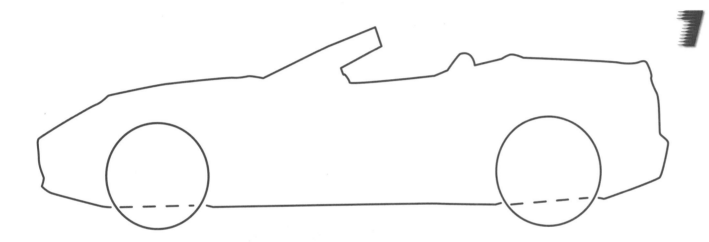

1 Draw the profile shape of this car and add two circles for the tires making sure you draw guidelines through the tire shapes.

2 Erase your guidelines and draw wheel wells, door, mirror, and lights. Also, draw seats and the windshield.

 Add contour details. Draw rims, trunk, tailpipe shape, and back lights.

Choose a ruby red with plenty of darks and lights. Add a tan interior and this Ferrari is ready to cruise.

Audi GT3 R8 Sports Car

The Audi's R8 is one of the fastest road cars in the world. But the customers demanded more, so the German car company built a race-prepped version. The Audi GT3 R8 is a tough endurance-racing car with 500 horsepower. Its body is designed for incredible handling in high-speed situations.

 Draw the simple shapes of the front grille, lights, and windshield glass. Add a line to the spoiler. Remember to draw the small shapes of the two front tires and erase any extra lines.

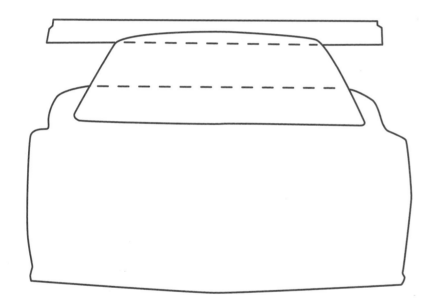

 Begin by sketching the basic shapes of the body, windshield, and spoiler (the piece at the back of the car). Draw through your shapes and then erase your guidelines.

 A charcoal gray is a great choice for the Audi GT. Use darker gray and black for the interior, spoiler, and grille, and you are off to the races!

 Use lines to show detail in the grille and headlights. Continue by adding mirrors, cockpit details, seats, and glass reflections.

Corvette

The Corvette has been a legendary sports car since 1953. This popular high performance vehicle makes it one of the finest and most fun-to-drive road vehicles today. It is often honored as the pace car for the world famous Indianapolis 500 race.

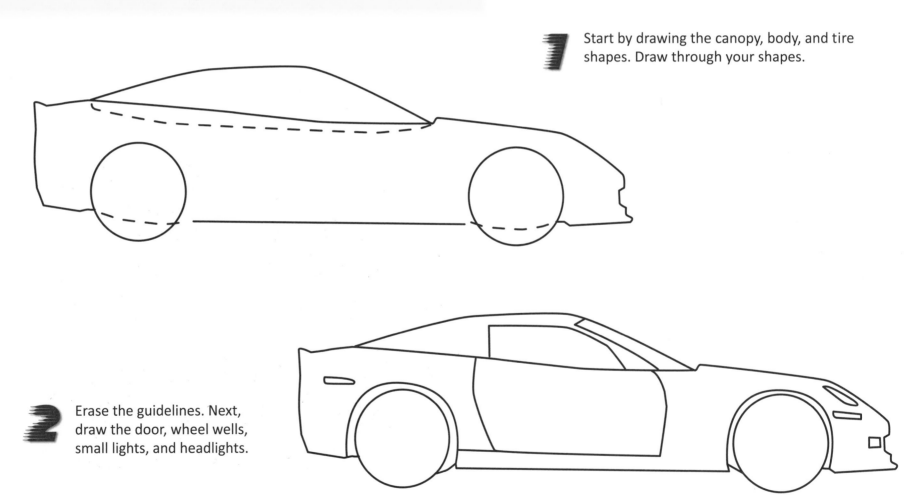

1 Start by drawing the canopy, body, and tire shapes. Draw through your shapes.

2 Erase the guidelines. Next, draw the door, wheel wells, small lights, and headlights.

Add rear window, mirrors, and rims. Use lines to show the body design.

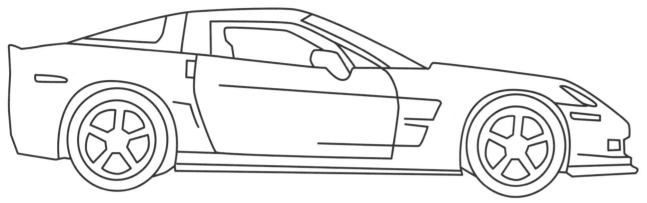

 This Vette looks good in purple. Add some highlights and some dark shading, a black back canopy, and this car is on its way.

Porsche Carrera GT

The Porsche Carrera GT is one of the ultimate super cars of all time. Built lightweight, with a powerful V10 engine, the Porsche Carrera GT can go faster than 200 miles per hour. This super cool roadster combines pure, brute power with incredible driving pleasure to support its reputation as a master in engineering.

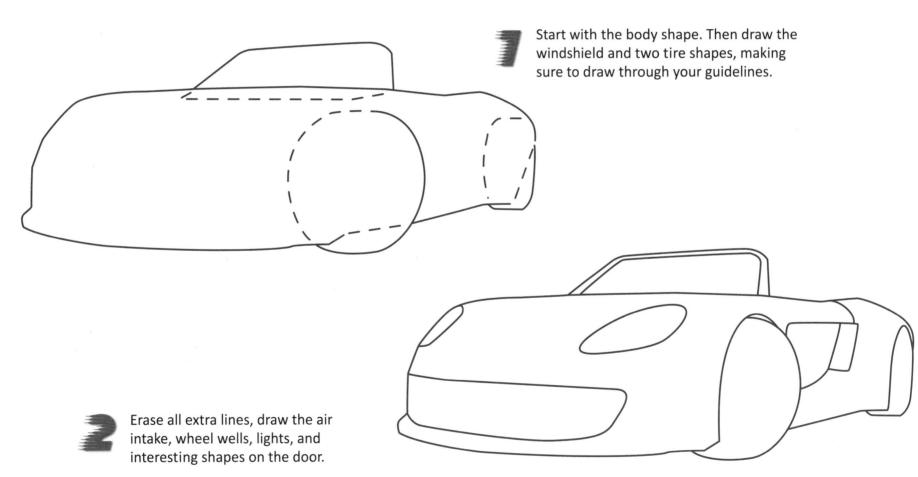

1 Start with the body shape. Then draw the windshield and two tire shapes, making sure to draw through your guidelines.

2 Erase all extra lines, draw the air intake, wheel wells, lights, and interesting shapes on the door.

 Draw seats, mirrors, and rear spoiler. Add the lights, rims, and front end details.

 A cool orange color with plenty of highlights and with black around the lights and front hood looks awesome. Add the black interior and make sure to add orange into the rims for the look that makes this Porsche ready to roll on the road.

Porsche Boxster

The German-manufactured Porsche Boxster is one of the most prestigious two-seater convertible roadsters ever. Its styling is inspired by the Porsche Carrera GT. The Boxster drives incredibly smooth, with a low center of gravity that gives its driver amazing high performance.

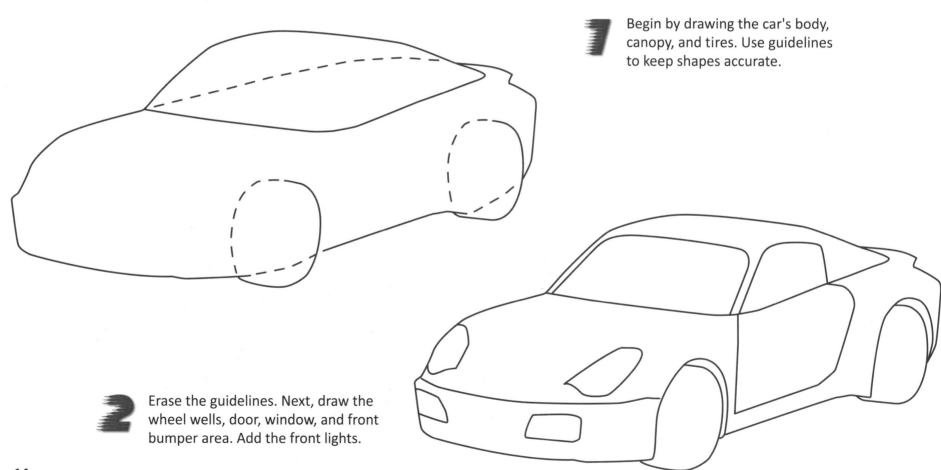

1 Begin by drawing the car's body, canopy, and tires. Use guidelines to keep shapes accurate.

2 Erase the guidelines. Next, draw the wheel wells, door, window, and front bumper area. Add the front lights.

 Draw interior details, glass door handle, and mirrors. Add hood detail and rims.

 A yellow base with light and dark shadowing and black around the lights looks great. Add the black interior color with some gray accents, and head out to the highway.

Maserati

Created in Italy by the Maserati brothers, the Maserati brand is well known for both its racing cars and sports cars. This famous line of luxury sports cars is built with a "passion for excellence" and extreme attention to details.

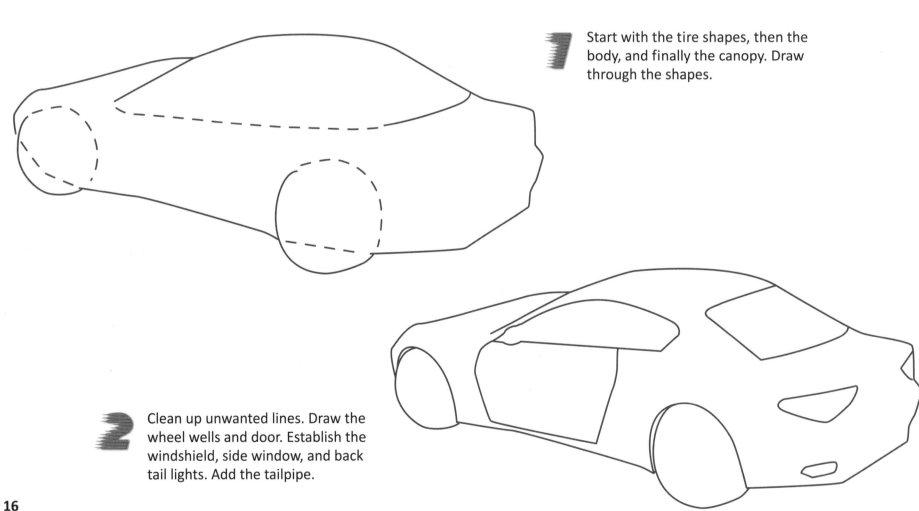

1 Start with the tire shapes, then the body, and finally the canopy. Draw through the shapes.

2 Clean up unwanted lines. Draw the wheel wells and door. Establish the windshield, side window, and back tail lights. Add the tailpipe.

 Add gas cap, mirror, door handle, and light details. Rim designs and bumper details come next. Use lines to show glass.

This Maserati is ready to take on the road with its highly reflective black color. Add deep red to the tail lights for that extra color.

Ford Mustang

The Ford Mustang created the "pony car"—a compact, uniquely styled car with long hoods and short rear decks. The car was introduced at the 1964 New York World's Fair.

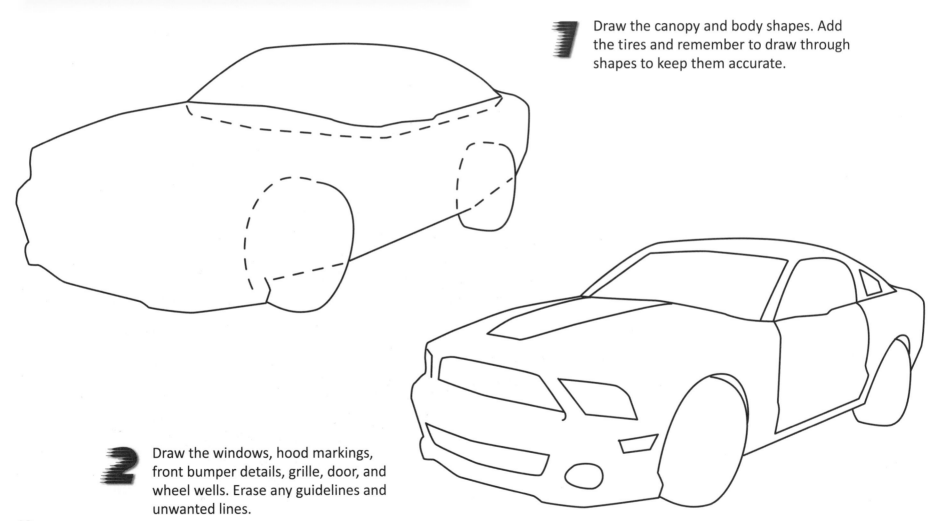

1 Draw the canopy and body shapes. Add the tires and remember to draw through shapes to keep them accurate.

2 Draw the windows, hood markings, front bumper details, grille, door, and wheel wells. Erase any guidelines and unwanted lines.

Add rims and mirrors. Use clean lines to establish the many planes that you see on the sides and hood areas.

 Choose a bright blue with some black and white stripes for this strong-looking Mustang. Go with dark windows and add yellow to the lights.

Ford Model T

The legendary Ford Model T was introduced by Henry Ford in 1908. As the world's first affordable motor car, it was known as the vehicle that "put America on wheels." When most people think of the first horseless carriages ever made, they picture in their mind the Ford Model T.

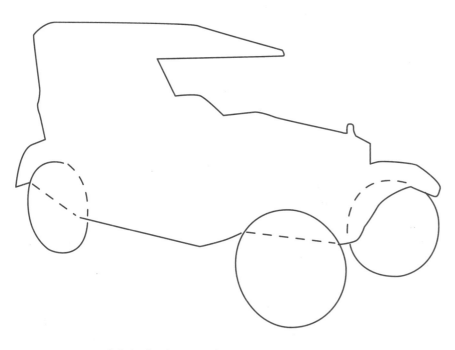

1 Establish the interesting shape of this antique car. Add the three visible tires and remember to draw through the shapes.

2 Erase unwanted lines and draw wheel wells, two doors, mirror, and running board. Draw front and back seats and the windshield. Add the steering wheel, back window, and canopy details.

 Add front grille and lights. Draw wheels and the spokes, making sure your lines are crisp and clean. Finally, draw the front axle.

 Forest green with black is a great combo for this classic Model T. Make sure to add some light green on the rims.

Smart Car

An extremely sub-compact vehicle, a Smart Car is one of the leaders in the pursuit of environmentally friendly electric cars. The original concept was to build a fun-to-drive and easy-to-park vehicle. Not much bigger than a golf cart, two Smart Cars can park in the same space as one regular-sized car.

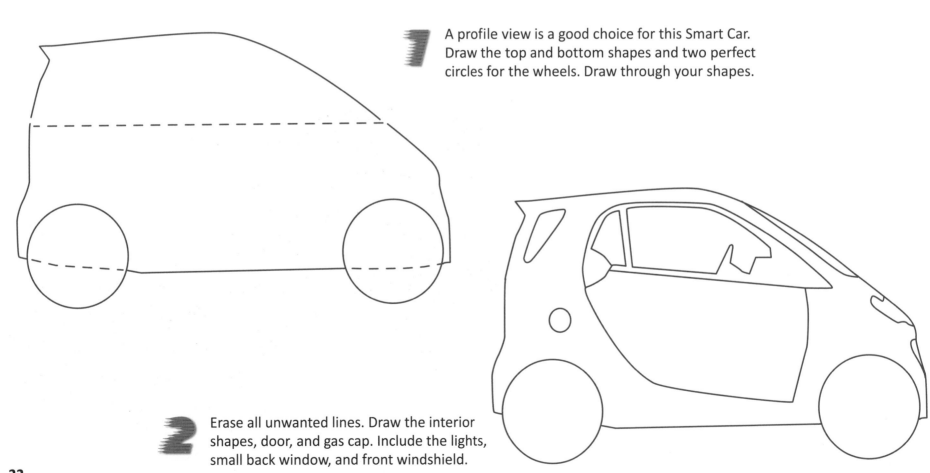

1 A profile view is a good choice for this Smart Car. Draw the top and bottom shapes and two perfect circles for the wheels. Draw through your shapes.

2 Erase all unwanted lines. Draw the interior shapes, door, and gas cap. Include the lights, small back window, and front windshield.

 Add back lights, side panel details, and tire rims.

Choose a two tone black and gray color for this Smart Car. Add reflections on the windows and red on the tail lights and you are ready to hit the road.

Formula One

The Formula One car is a single-seat, open cockpit race car with large front and rear wings. The engine is positioned right behind the driver. Formula One racing is the highest class of racing and has a giant TV audience of over 600 million viewers per season.

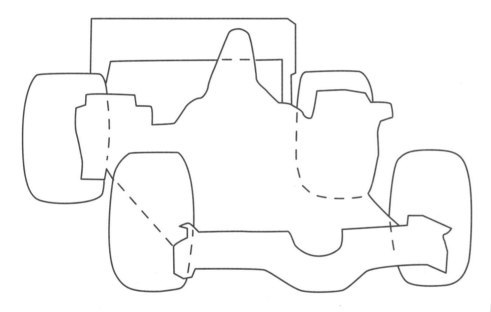

 Draw the overall shape of this unique looking race car. Add all four large tire shapes. Draw through shapes to keep them looking correct. Add the big spoiler in the back.

 Clean up your guidelines. Add mirrors, cockpit, air intakes, and spoiler supports.

 Draw rims and additional spoiler details. Use lines to establish contours. Add the tire supports and the number "1" on the front.

This Formula One will look great in red. Make sure there is contrast in the tires to show the treads. Finish it off with a yellow number "1"—it is a winning combination for sure.

Pickup Truck

A pickup truck is a light motor vehicle with an open-top rear cargo bed, which is almost always separated from the cab. This tough vehicle has the durability to carry heavy loads. The very first pickup premiered in 1925, and was based on the Ford Model T car.

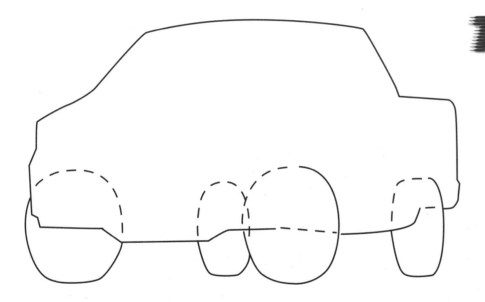

1 Draw the overall shape of the truck. Add all four tires and remember to draw through shapes to keep them accurate.

2 Establish the windows, hood markings, front bumper, and grille. Add the door, mirrors, and wheel wells. Remove any unwanted lines.

 Draw rims and additional lights. Use lines to establish the interior shapes and front end details.

 This Ford truck will look great with a medium blue and silver combo. Make sure to add nice highlights to the chrome bumper and darken the windows.

Muscle Car

A muscle car is a small, two-door car from the 1960s loaded with a big powerful engine. It is driven as a street car and used in professional drag racing events. When you hear a big rumbling on the road, there's a good chance a muscle car is nearby.

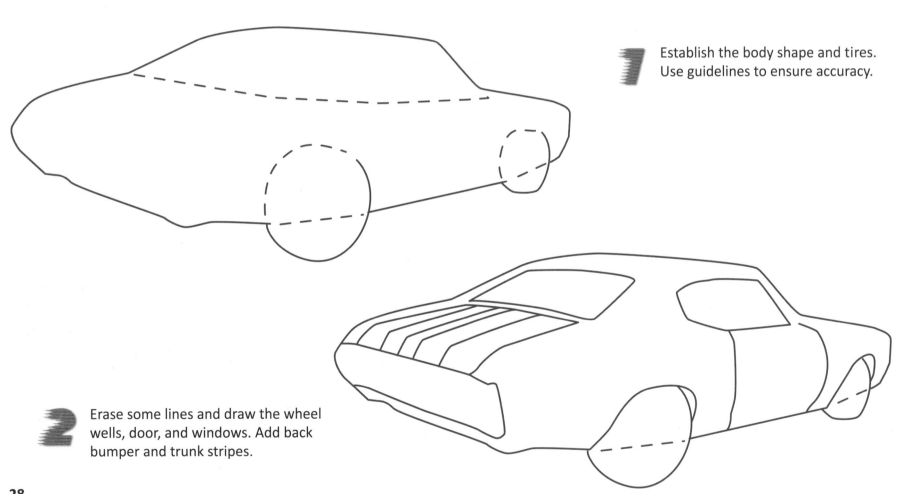

1 Establish the body shape and tires. Use guidelines to ensure accuracy.

2 Erase some lines and draw the wheel wells, door, and windows. Add back bumper and trunk stripes.

 Draw door handle, mirror, cool rims, lights, and tailpipes. Add lines for glass and body structure. Erase remaining unwanted lines.

 This muscle car looks great in purple with white stripes. Add highlights for reflections and chrome for the bumper and tailpipes. Make sure to use some details on the rims. This car is ready to flex some muscles on the road!

Racing Car

Blazing fast speeds, ultimate maneuverability, and perfect precision are the qualities that make a great racing car. Knowing how the racing car is constructed is one of the most important aspects of becoming a great race driver.

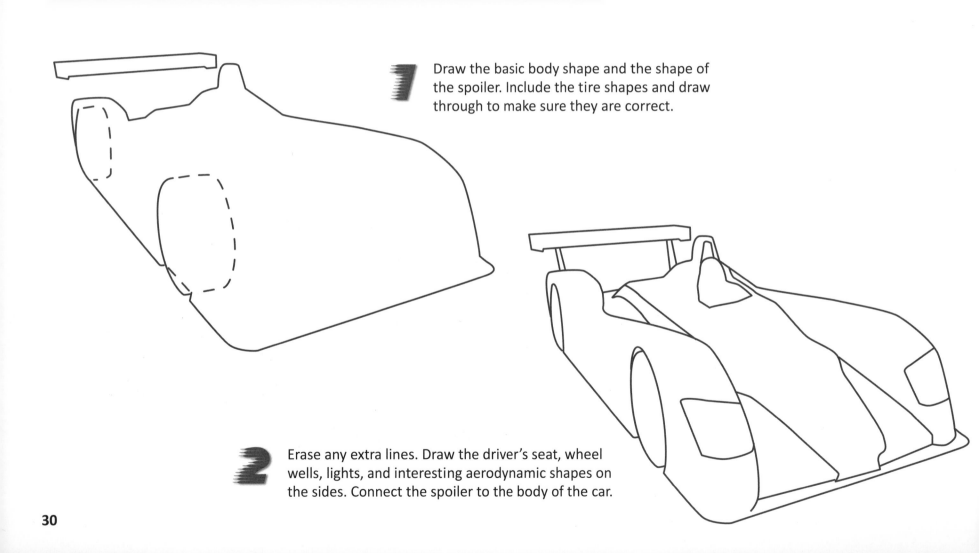

1 Draw the basic body shape and the shape of the spoiler. Include the tire shapes and draw through to make sure they are correct.

2 Erase any extra lines. Draw the driver's seat, wheel wells, lights, and interesting aerodynamic shapes on the sides. Connect the spoiler to the body of the car.

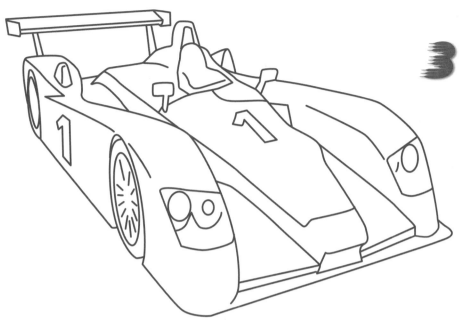

 Draw mirrors, rims, air intakes, and other details. Add a number to the hood.

A silver and red color combination is a great choice for this car. Make sure you blend the red into the silver for an extra cool look. This car is ready to win the race!

Dodge Viper

The Dodge Viper is a powerful vehicle, inspired by the classic American sports car. Its bold hood, with signature racing stripes, has made it a very popular vehicle for TV shows, movies, and video games.

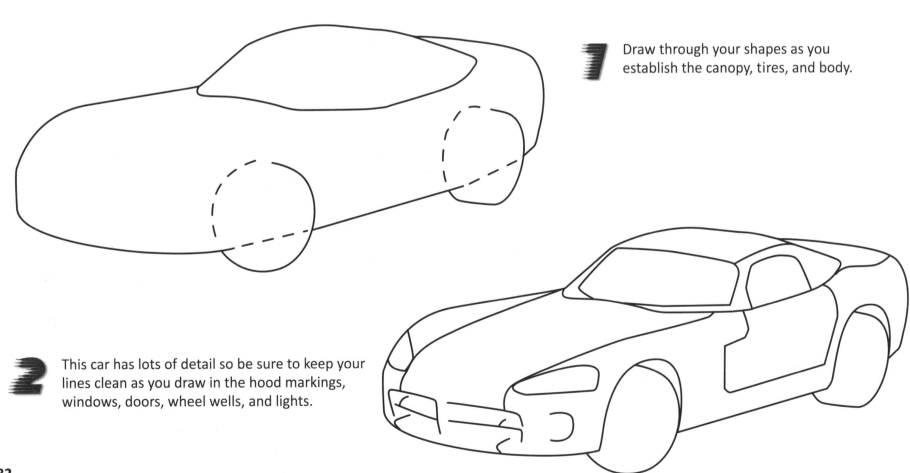

1 Draw through your shapes as you establish the canopy, tires, and body.

2 This car has lots of detail so be sure to keep your lines clean as you draw in the hood markings, windows, doors, wheel wells, and lights.

 Add details to the hood. Draw mirrors, side contours, rims, and interior shapes.

 Red with a black center stripe will bring lots of attention to this Viper. Add plenty of highlights to the body and windows, and you are good to go.

Audi

Audi is a brand of German-engineered luxury vehicles known for its style and sports-driven beauty. Audi shows off its superior engineering by holding multiple world records for endurance racing.

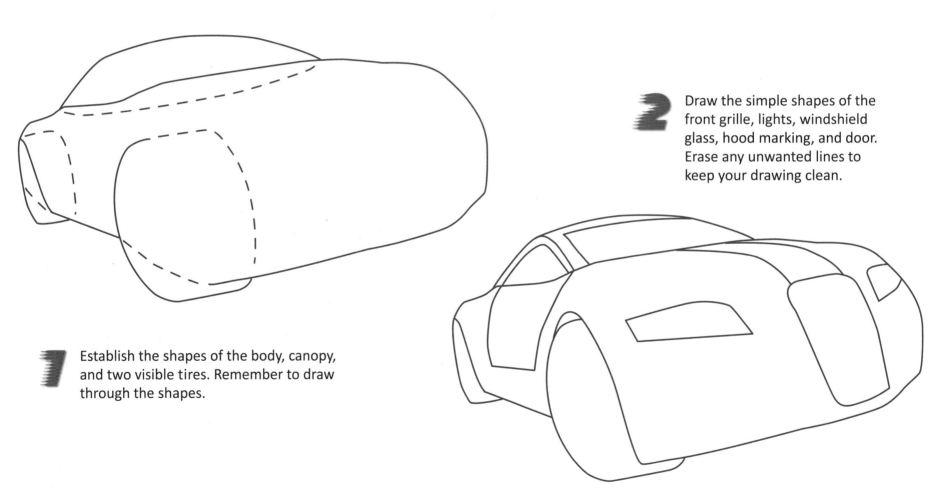

2 Draw the simple shapes of the front grille, lights, windshield glass, hood marking, and door. Erase any unwanted lines to keep your drawing clean.

1 Establish the shapes of the body, canopy, and two visible tires. Remember to draw through the shapes.

 Use lines to show the contour of the body. Add driver side window, mirror, and rim details. Add depth to the grille.

 Use a rich red color for the basic color with black and white markings for contrast. Add highlights and darker tones on the rims. Your Audi is now complete!

Aston Martin

Aston Martin is a British manufacturer with a classic reputation, as well as being a modern luxury sports car. It has been a favorite vehicle for secret agents in several movies.

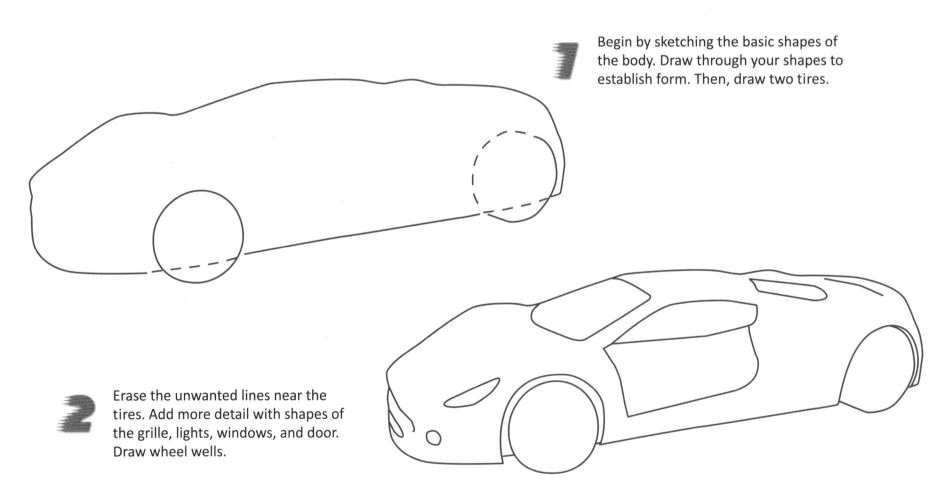

1 Begin by sketching the basic shapes of the body. Draw through your shapes to establish form. Then, draw two tires.

2 Erase the unwanted lines near the tires. Add more detail with shapes of the grille, lights, windows, and door. Draw wheel wells.

 Continue by adding more detail with crisp clean lines. Add mirrors and cockpit details. Draw the cool rims and use lines to show form on the hood and side panel.

 Choose a gold color for your Aston Martin and a black for the interior. Show shadows and reflections with a darker tone, and add highlights with lighter tones. Finish off the rims and hit the road!

Lotus Elise

The Lotus Elise premiered in 1996 as a rear-wheel drive roadster. A Lotus Elise is built to be extremely lightweight in order to achieve amazing performance and speed.

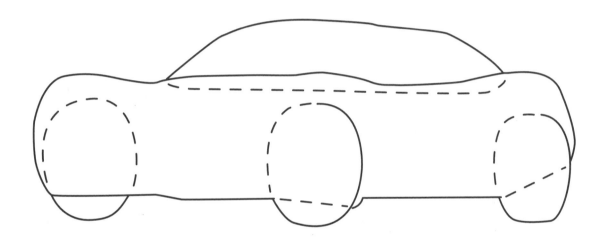

 Draw the two basic shapes of the car and the three visible tires. Draw through the shapes where they overlap.

 Erase any unwanted lines. Draw wheel wells, mirror, and door. Establish the windshield lights and other hood shapes.

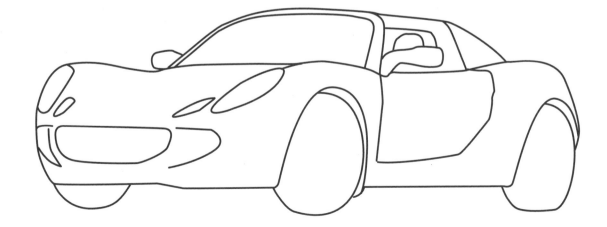

3 Add the rims and continue working on the hood shape. Use lines to show all the air intake features. Draw the small lights and glass.

 A bright orange will certainly make this Lotus stand out in a crowd. Go with black rims and interior. Add yellow highlights and off you go!

McLaren F1

The McLaren F1 is lighter and more streamlined than most of the sports car rivals in its class. The driver's seat is located in the middle of the vehicle. The use of Formula One-inspired technology makes it one of the finest and fastest cars on the road.

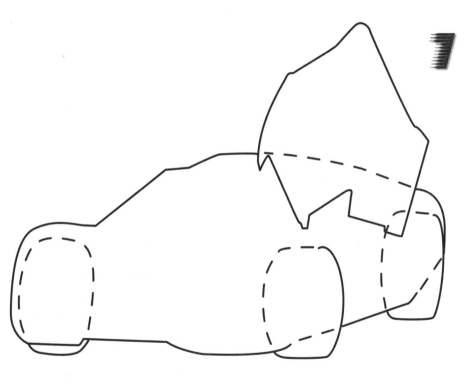

1 Start with the door shape, then the body, and finally the three tires. Remember to draw through your shapes.

2 Erase any unwanted lines. Add detail to the door with the mirror and glass. Draw the spoiler, headlights, and windshield. Don't forget the other mirror.

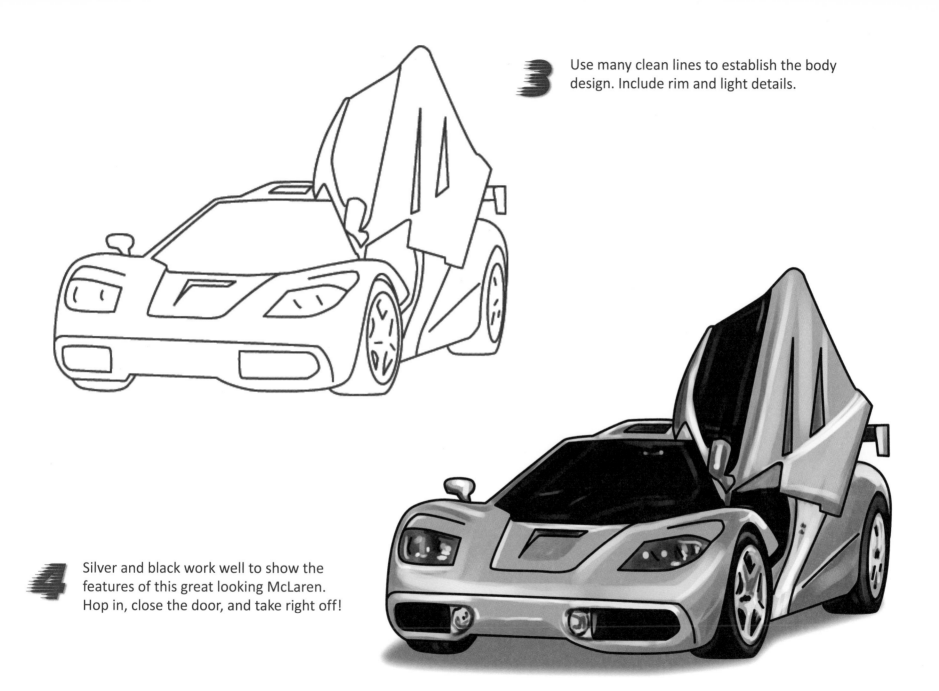

3 Use many clean lines to establish the body design. Include rim and light details.

4 Silver and black work well to show the features of this great looking McLaren. Hop in, close the door, and take right off!

NASCAR Stock Car

Unlike a racing car designed from the ground up for speed, the stock car looks like a regular American family car, but it is built to meet a strict set of NASCAR regulations. The suspension and engine are the same on all vehicles for fair, but fierce, competition.

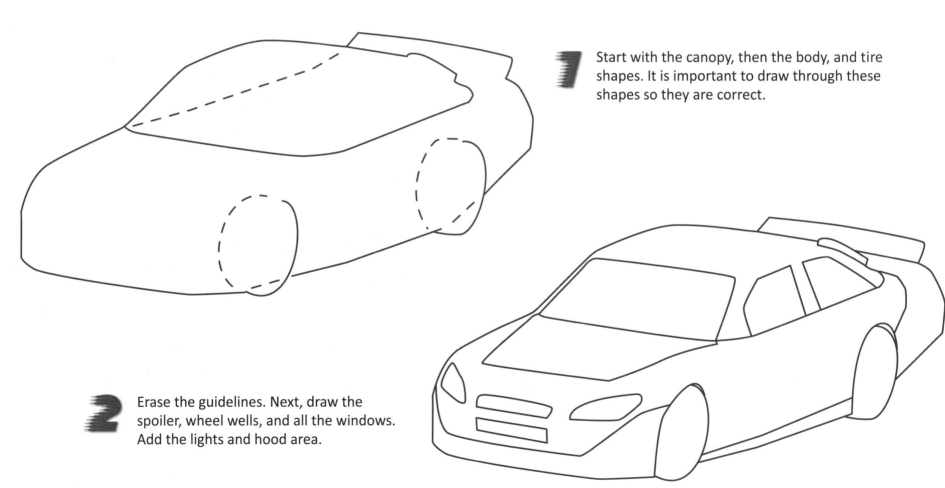

1 Start with the canopy, then the body, and tire shapes. It is important to draw through these shapes so they are correct.

2 Erase the guidelines. Next, draw the spoiler, wheel wells, and all the windows. Add the lights and hood area.

 Use nice, clean ellipse shapes for the rims. Add the racing number on the top and door. Add lines on the windshield.

NASCAR cars have lots of fun color in them, so go wild and show as much color as you want! This yellow and red combo will win the race for sure!

Cadillac XLR-V

The Cadillac XLR-V convertible takes the Cadillac two-seat convertible to new levels. It is a very comfortable luxury car, while at the same time capable of incredible speed and power.

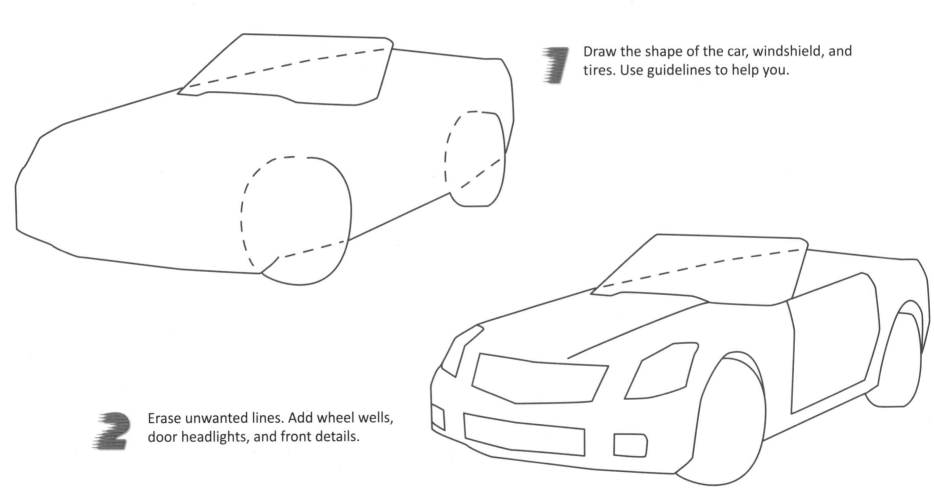

1 Draw the shape of the car, windshield, and tires. Use guidelines to help you.

2 Erase unwanted lines. Add wheel wells, door headlights, and front details.

 Add seats, glass, and mirrors. Next, draw the rims, gas cap, and lines on the hood.

 A pearl white color will work well here. Use dark and light shading for highlights. Make sure to add some highlights to the black interior. Now you can ride in style!

De Tomaso Pantera

The De Tomaso Pantera is a classically styled Italian car commonly powered by a Ford engine. The word Pantera translates to "panther," perfectly describing its sleek design. It was one of the favorite cars owned by the King of Rock and Roll, Elvis Presley.

1 Draw the shape of the body and the roof remembering to draw through with guidelines. Add two perfect circles for the tires.

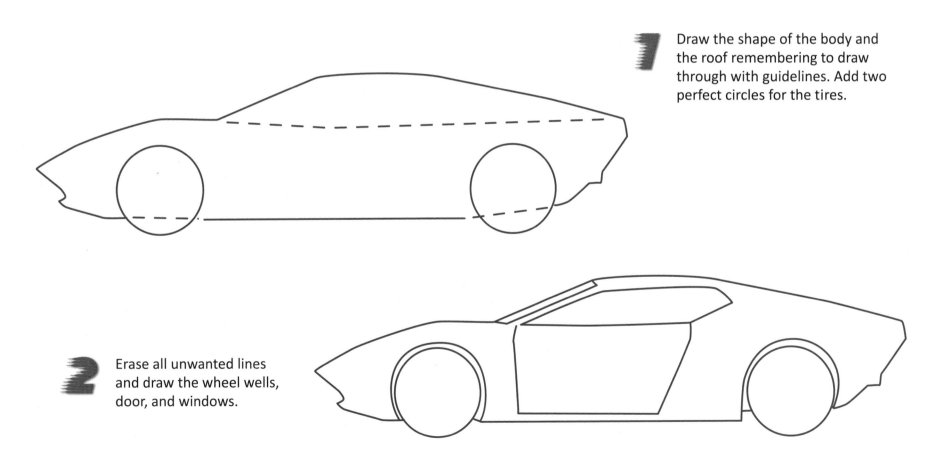

2 Erase all unwanted lines and draw the wheel wells, door, and windows.

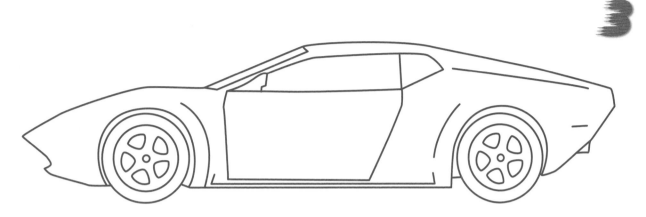

3 Draw a tailpipe, mirror, and a small side window. Do not forget the rims and body contour lines.

4 Choose a bright lime green color and add shading. Go with dark glass and a black stripe on the bottom of the car for a powerful contrast. This cool car will surely be noticed on the road.

Jaguar XJ

The Jaguar XJ is a spacious four-door luxury car. The British XJ was launched in 1968 and is still one of the hottest cars on the road today. A unique feature on the car is its twin fuel tanks, positioned on each side of the trunk.

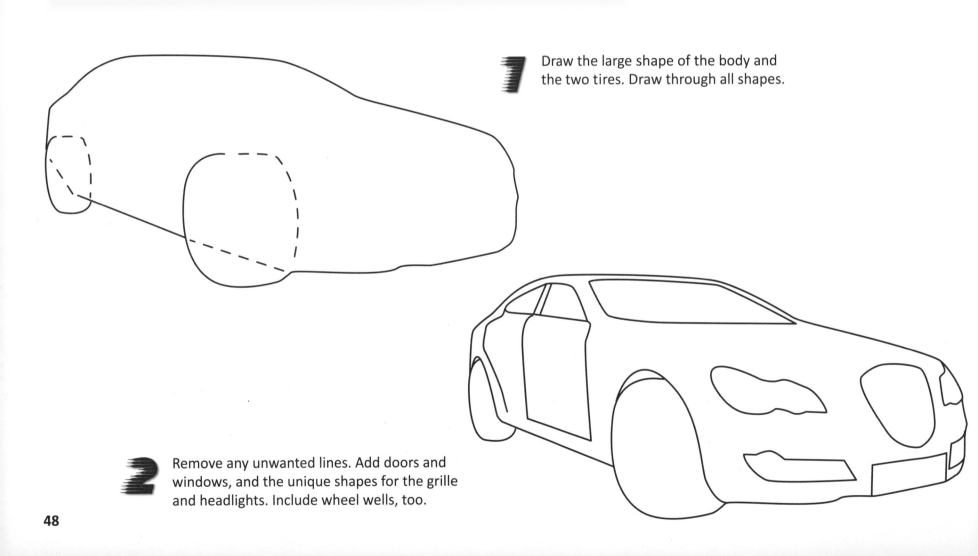

1 Draw the large shape of the body and the two tires. Draw through all shapes.

2 Remove any unwanted lines. Add doors and windows, and the unique shapes for the grille and headlights. Include wheel wells, too.

3 Draw the rims and door details. Add the mirrors and hood, as well as the small lights.

4 This Jaguar will look beautiful on the city streets in a rich red color. Add highlights and dark shadows. Make sure the chrome is shining.

Tesla Roadster Sport

The Tesla Roadster Sport debuted in 2009. It is an unbelievably high-performance, electric sports car. The sleek, stylized Roadster can travel 244 miles on a single charge of its ground-breaking battery pack. It can go 0 to 60 in 3.9 seconds and has a top speed of 125 mph on pure electric power.

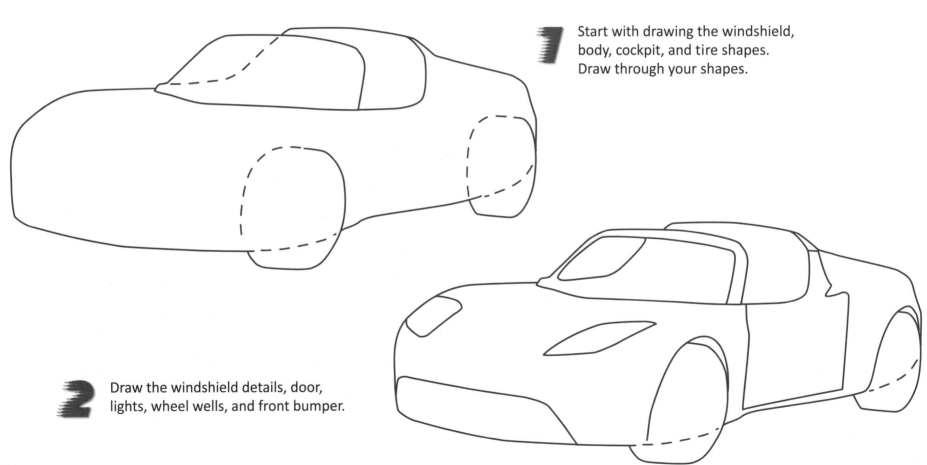

1 Start with drawing the windshield, body, cockpit, and tire shapes. Draw through your shapes.

2 Draw the windshield details, door, lights, wheel wells, and front bumper.

 Add seats, gas cap, and contour lines. Draw tire rims.

 Go with a nice bright red color. Add some yellow highlights with black interior and this Tesla will cruise with style.

Koenigsegg CCX

The Swedish-made Koenigsegg model CCX is a supercar with a unique aerodynamic shape designed for strength and flowing motion. It is engineered with the goal of ultimate power.

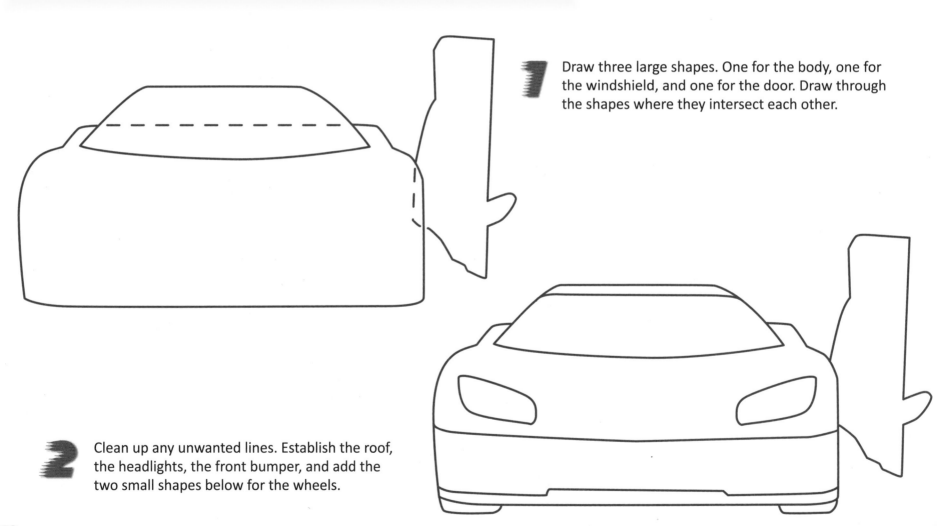

1 Draw three large shapes. One for the body, one for the windshield, and one for the door. Draw through the shapes where they intersect each other.

2 Clean up any unwanted lines. Establish the roof, the headlights, the front bumper, and add the two small shapes below for the wheels.

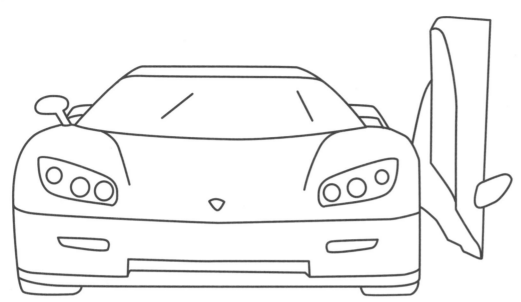

 Finish the door details. Add the mirrors, lines for the hood, and air intakes, as well as the small lights. Use lines to show windshield glass.

 Choose a deep red color for this futuristic-looking machine. Add silver to the bumper and go with dark tinted glass, and this Koenigsegg is ready to take off!

Pagani Zonda

The Italian-made Pagani Zonda debuted in 1999. As of 2009, there are barely more than one hundred built. One of the rarest, most exclusive cars on the planet, this ultra-cool sports car is currently stealing the spotlight at top auto shows.

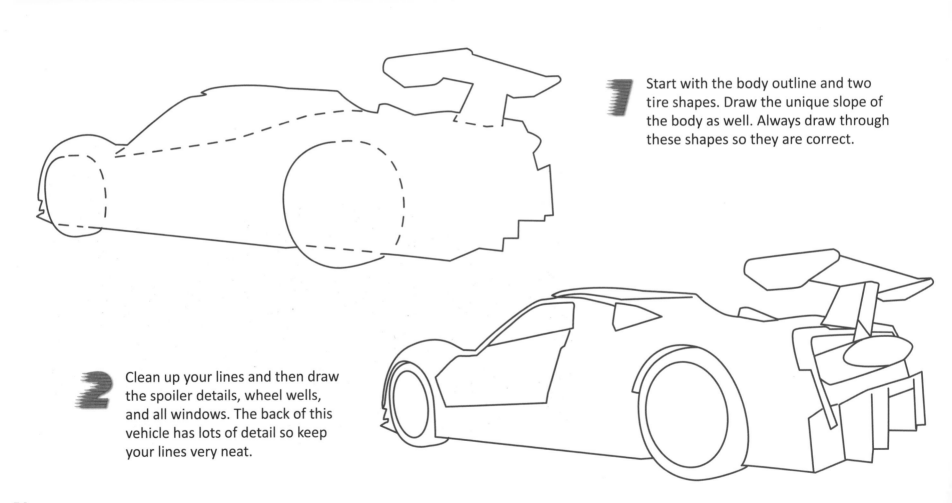

1 Start with the body outline and two tire shapes. Draw the unique slope of the body as well. Always draw through these shapes so they are correct.

2 Clean up your lines and then draw the spoiler details, wheel wells, and all windows. The back of this vehicle has lots of detail so keep your lines very neat.

 Next, add the rim detail and the mirror. Use clean crisp lines to show the side design. Finish by adding more detail to the back area.

 A black and silver color combo gives this Pagani a nice presence on the road! Add a bit of orange to the tail lights and it is finished.

Peugeot RCZ

The Peugeot RCZ is designed with a stunning, almost triangular shape. It is a luxurious lifestyle vehicle that is pure driving fun.

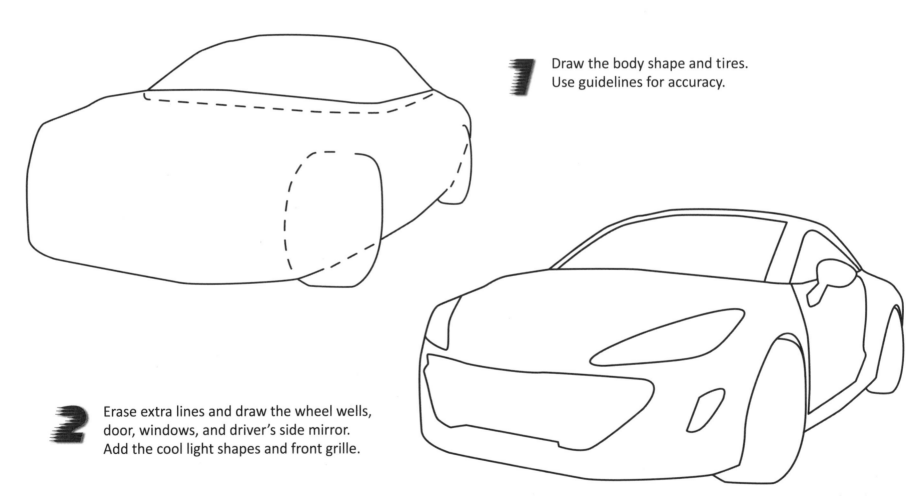

1 Draw the body shape and tires. Use guidelines for accuracy.

2 Erase extra lines and draw the wheel wells, door, windows, and driver's side mirror. Add the cool light shapes and front grille.

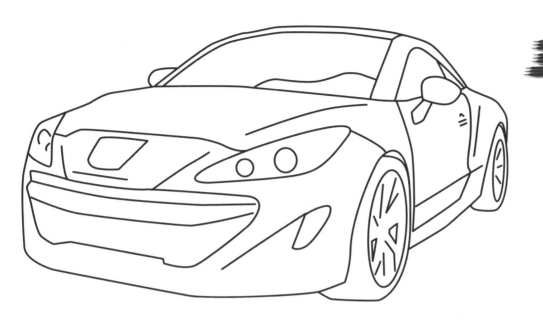

 Draw the rims, grille details, hood contours, and cockpit shape. Finally, add the passenger side mirror.

A midnight blue color is great for this Peugeot with plenty of highlights and dark contrasts. Add the rich red interior color and it is ready for the road.

Bugatti Veyon

The Bugatti Veyon may be the fastest production vehicle of all time. It is a super car built around a monster 1,001 horsepower engine for a top speed of more than 250 mph.

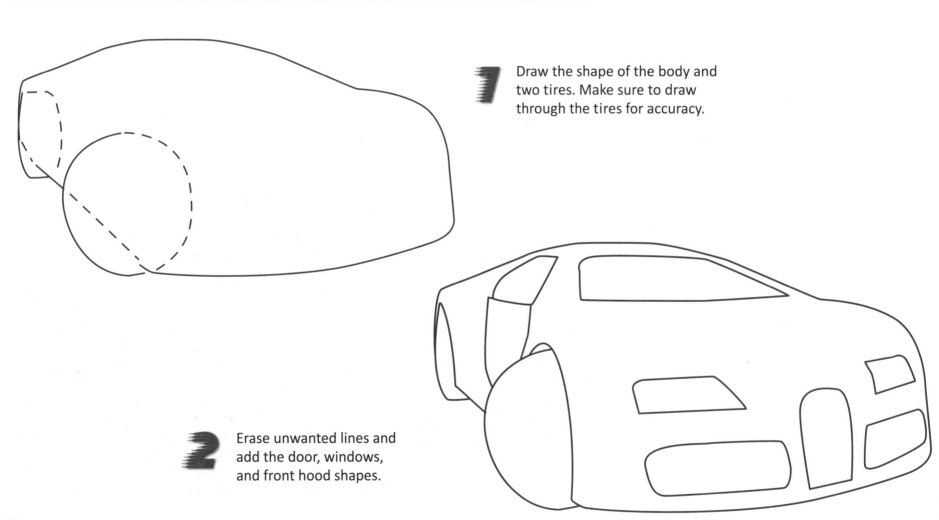

1 Draw the shape of the body and two tires. Make sure to draw through the tires for accuracy.

2 Erase unwanted lines and add the door, windows, and front hood shapes.

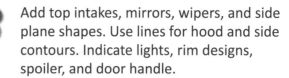 Add top intakes, mirrors, wipers, and side plane shapes. Use lines for hood and side contours. Indicate lights, rim designs, spoiler, and door handle.

 Choose a two tone blue for this beautiful Bugatti. Use a mixture of darks and lights and add a few orange highlights to spice it up. Make sure to add blue reflections in the rims.

Camaro

The Chevrolet Camaro is a pony car that was unleashed to the public in 1966. Although the vehicle was temporarily out of production after 2002, it came roaring back onto the road slick and more fun to drive than ever.

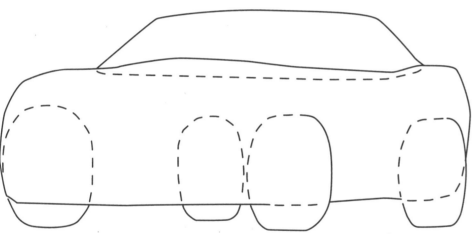

 Erase some unwanted lines. Begin to add more detail with shapes of the grille, small lights, windshield, and door. Draw wheel wells and hood markings.

1 Begin by sketching the basic shapes of the body and roof. Draw through the shapes to establish form. Then, draw all four tires.

 Continue by adding detail with crisp clean lines and erase any remaining unwanted lines. Add mirrors, headlights, and cockpit details. Add the cool rims, and use lines to show form on the hood and side panel.

 Finish your Camaro by adding a yellow base color. Paint in shadows and reflections with a darker tone and add highlights with lighter tones. Now your Camaro is ready to roll!

Monster Truck

The monster truck is a kind of vehicle that is modified with oversized wheels and suspension, designed to crush smaller vehicles beneath its massive tires. Monster truck sporting events thrill fans with tricks such as wheel stands and jumps.

 This monster truck starts with one basic body shape and four huge tire shapes. It is important to draw through those tire shapes so they are correct.

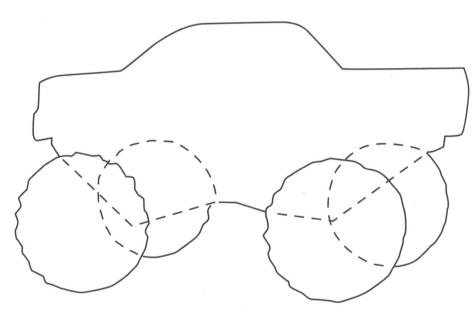

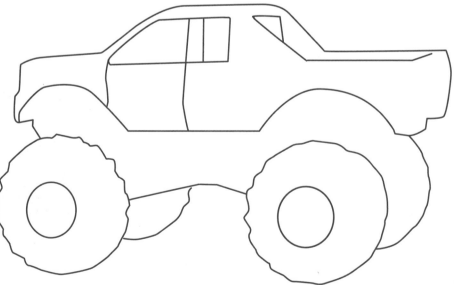

 Establish the body by drawing the wheel wells, the truck bed, windows, and doors. Erase any unwanted lines to clean up the wheels and add rims.

 Use lines to show tire treads and the giant shocks. Show chassis and rim details and add some cool graphics on the side.

 Use a bright red and yellow color combination and make sure you show plenty of highlights on the big treads! This monster truck looks like it can roll over anything!